ANGER MANAGEMENT FOR COUPLES:

What You Need to Know and How to Manage It

By

Hallel Isaac

COPYRIGHT

TABLE OF CONTENTS

Table of Contents

INTRODUCTION

Anger is a healthy and common human emotion that often surfaces in relationships, even when it is not directed towards the recipient of the expression. Unfortunately, when we engage with the people we love the most, especially our romantic relationships, rage frequently makes an appearance. However, being passionate in a relationship shouldn't lead to the outburst of strong emotions like wrath. In any romantic relationship, being able to control your anger and how you react to an angry partner is a crucial skill that can foster intimacy and maturity.

Since the importance of handling anger in relationships wisely cannot be overstated, understanding and controlling anger (anger management) in relationships are the main focus of this book.

CHAPTER 1

WHAT IS ANGER?

Everyone occasionally feels angry, which is a natural feeling even if it can be unwelcome or unreasonable.

According to experts on anger, the feeling is a basic, natural one that has developed as a defense mechanism against what is viewed as wrongdoing.

We are more prone to feel angry if our basic needs (food, shelter, sex, sleep, etc.) are not provided or are jeopardized in some manner. Mild anger may be brought on by feeling fatigued, pressured, or irritated.

It's possible for humans to get furious in response to irritation, criticism, or a threat, and this emotion is not always undesirable or wrong.

Our capacity to communicate successfully can be hampered by anger, which increases our propensity to say or do inappropriate or irrational things. We can also be irritated by the beliefs, ideas, and actions of other people.

Effective communication can be hampered by being unreasonable or irrational since it makes those around us feel frightened, resentful, or furious.

HOW ANGER IS EXPRESSED

Different sorts of anger affect people differently and can emerge to produce various acts and signals of rage. Anger can be communicated in a variety of ways. Both vocal and nonverbal expressions of rage are frequently seen.

Someone's anger may be evident in their tone of voice, what they say, or how they express it. Anger can also be conveyed nonverbally and through body language, such as trying to appear physically larger and so scary, glaring, frowning, and fist-clenching. Some people are quite skilled at repressing their anger within, so it could be challenging to spot any outward manifestations. However, it is uncommon for a real physical attack to occur without any 'warning' signals beforehand.

WHAT MAKES PEOPLE ANGRY?

At a primal intuitive level, rage can be utilized to defend one's home or family, secure or protect one's mate's rights, safeguard against losing food or other assets, or react to other perceived threats.

CHAPTER 2

RECOGNISING ANGER IN YOURSELF AND OTHERS

There are often both physical and emotional symptoms to anger and, by recognizing these, you are more likely to be able to control them.

Possible Physical Signs of Anger:

- Frequent rubbing of the face.

- Tightly clasping one hand with the other, or making clenched fists.

- Clenching of the jaw or grinding teeth.

- Shallow breathing and/or breathlessness.

- Increased heart-rate.

- Perspiring, sweaty palms.

- Trembling or shaking lips, hands.

- Rocking motion whilst sitting.

- Pacing.

- Being rude and losing sense of humor.

- Talking louder.

- Increased cravings for tobacco, sugar, alcohol, drugs, comfort food etc.

Possible Emotional Symptoms of Anger

- A desire to 'run away' from the situation.

- Irritation.

- Feeling sad or depressed.

- Felling guilty or resentful.

- Anxiety, feeling anxious can manifest in many different ways.

- A feeling or desire to lash out verbally or physically.

CAN ANGER MAKE YOU ILL?

When we are angry, our bodies release the hormones adrenaline and cortisol, the same hormones released when we encounter stress.

As a result of these releases in hormones our blood pressure, pulse, body temperature and breathing rate may increase, sometimes to potentially dangerous levels. This natural chemical reaction is designed to give us an instant boost of energy and power and is often referred to as the 'fight or flight' reaction. This means that the body and mind prepare for a fight or for running away from danger.

However, people who get angry often cannot manage their anger effectively and can become ill, just as stress that is left unresolved may make you ill. Our bodies are not designed to withstand high levels of adrenaline and cortisol over long periods or on a very regular basis.

Some of the health problems that may occur as a result of being angry regularly or for long periods of time can include:

- Aches and pains, usually in the back and head.

- High blood pressure, which can, in severe cases, lead to serious complaints such as stroke or cardiac arrest.

- Sleep problems.

- Problems with digestion.

- Skin disorders.

- Reduced threshold for pain.

- Impaired immune system.

Anger can also lead to psychological problems such as:

- Depression.

- Reduced self confidence.

- Eating disorders.

- Alcoholism.

- Substance abuse.

- Self-injury.

CHAPTER 3

TYPE OF ANGER ISSUES

1. Assertive Anger

Anger expressed assertively is regarded as being positive. Assertive rage is utilized as a healthy and constructive way to communicate irritation in order to bring about positive change, as opposed to avoiding conversations or having frequent fits of screaming or yelling.

A healthy, safe means of expressing your feelings can be the appearance of assertive fury. You might begin a sentence with, "I feel angry when..." or "I think..." as an example. Anger that is assertive is often accompanied by appropriate body language and, perhaps, expectations about how to handle or process the event. You now have the option to vent your rage in a way that encourages constructive change.

2. Behavioral Anger

Men with anger issues frequently exhibit behavioral anger, which is a physical reaction. This is a risk because it might erupt violently, possibly devolving into destructive or displaced anger. Behavioral rage is impulsive and unpredictable, and it can occasionally have negative social or legal repercussions.

Intimidating actions (such as cornering someone or raising your voice), pushing or throwing objects, smashing objects, or attacking someone are all examples of behavioral anger. Determining if your rage is moving into this territory as a result of possible interpersonal or legal repercussions is crucial.

3. Chronic Anger

Chronic anger often targets other people, situations, and even oneself, which can lower one's sense of self-worth. It can occasionally do significant harm while while flying under the radar.

A constant, low-level feeling of rage, bitterness, impatience, and exasperation is what chronic anger feels like. It can apply to other people, particular circumstances, or yourself, as was already established. Because of how you experience anger, you could find it difficult to understand and communicate your demands, which can have an adverse effect on your relationships, stress levels, and general well-being.

4. Destructive Anger

Anger that is destructive in nature is a very unhealthy emotion that can have a variety of detrimental effects. This sort of anger is frequently associated with the extreme end of behavioral anger, despite the paucity of study on it. Extreme anger or even hatred for other people, even when it is unjustified, may fall under this category.

Destructive rage can manifest as acts (such as tossing and damaging things that are valuable to the person you're furious with) or words used to harm others. This can occasionally manifest in relationships as stonewalling (i.e., shutting out your significant other emotionally). Destructive rage has the capacity to ruin significant social connections and have a very bad impact on many aspects of your life.

5. Judgmental Anger

Judgmental rage frequently results from a perceived affront, another person's defects (if you believe they have an impact on you), or an injustice committed against you or another person. People who have judgmental anger are known to have core beliefs (a fundamental viewpoint or knowledge of the world), typically one that makes them feel superior to or inferior to others, which makes them criticize them and feel furious about their behaviors or expressions.

When you or another person gets upset because of what you or they feel to be an injustice or slight, this is what is commonly referred to as "justifiable fury." This kind of rage can also manifest itself in the form of insulting others or yelling over a perceived injustice. This may make it more difficult for you to maintain a support network and may have a negative effect on how you interact with others. Additionally, you might feel lonely and have low self-esteem.

6. Overwhelmed Anger

Anger overload can have unanticipated long-term effects on your mental well-being. Particularly when you don't discover means to express or articulate how you feel, this kind of fury festers. It might become apparent when things reach a "boiling point" or when your capacity to handle stress and fury has been exceeded as a result of specific circumstances, emotions, or relationships.

Overwhelmed rage can appear as a sharp burst of annoyance and hostility after a protracted period of restraint. Everybody's expression of overpowering rage is distinct, but it always manifests unexpectedly and may be accompanied by a stressful incident.

7. Passive-Aggressive Anger

An expression of avoidance, passive aggression is fury. This form of fury arises when you try to avoid all disputes and repress your emotions. Because anger frequently affects your self-esteem levels, it might be dangerous. Because of this, passive-aggressive anger may harm your relationships.

Emotional suppression and conflict avoidance are both characteristics of passive-aggressive fury, which can be verbal or physical. Sarcasm, passive-aggressive remarks (such as "I like your dress, even though it doesn't fit you"), or a purposeful lack of response can all be used to convey this. The vocal manifestation of passive aggressiveness is the most frequent, but it can also take the form of closed-off body language or persistent procrastination at work.

8. Retaliatory Anger

It's normal and natural to feel angry in retaliation after being attacked. It could be inspired by a desire for vengeance following a perceived wrong.

This form of fury is typically intended to harm the person who injured you. A desire to exert control over an occurrence may have an impact. When you experience verbal or physical abuse, you could find yourself directing your rage at particular persons. Retaliatory rage has the potential to make relationships more uncomfortable and angrier.

9. Self-Abusive Anger

Embarrassment is frequently associated with self-abusive fury. People who have low self-esteem or who feel hopeless and unworthy exhibit this form of fury. Self-abusive rage is frequently employed as a coping mechanism, despite the fact that it simply serves to drive people more apart.

Anger directed against oneself can have both internal and outward effects. It may manifest as self-harming behavior, alcohol or drug abuse, unhealthful and disordered eating, or negative self-talk (such as "You are a failure"). It can also take the form of internalizing bad emotions and acting them out on oneself. Externally, this could appear as verbal abuse or lash outs at other people.

10. Silent Anger

An internal, non-verbal manner of expressing rage is through silence. Even if you don't express your anger out loud, others can still be able to tell. Silent fury is often suppressed and allowed to build up inside of a person, which can cause stress, tension, and behaviors indicative of overwhelmed rage.

An internal or outward experience of silent fury is possible. This kind of internal fury can lead to a buildup of unspoken dissatisfaction, anger, and resentment, which can lead to excessive stress and low levels of continuing tension. Externally, it may manifest as restrained or minimal speech and tone, as well as closed-off body language and facial expression.

11. Verbal Anger

Anger expressed verbally can turn violent and be abusive. It has been observed that people who experience this kind of fury feel regret after attacking the object of their rage and may even repent after an incident.

Verbal rage can manifest as verbal abuse or "going off" on someone. Loud shouting, threatening actions, snide remarks, relentless and harsh criticism, and ridiculing are only a few examples of specific behaviors. Recall that verbal rage can escalate into verbal abuse. Additionally, it may make it difficult for you to keep up solid or healthy connections.

12. Volatile Anger

Volatile anger, often known as "sudden fury," is an explosive form of rage. It can occur when someone is irritated, no matter how tiny, and loses control, erupting verbally or physically and possibly inflicting harm. The person finds it difficult to explain, think about, and communicate when they are angry like this.

Volatile anger might appear as a quick transition from acceptance of the status quo to wrath over actual or imagined slights. It is frequently destructive and includes physical hostility, yelling, throwing objects, and shouting. You might not be able to keep up dependable connections if you are angry like this.

CHAPTER 4

ANGER IN RELATIONSHIP

One of the hardest, and frequently terrifying,

 emotions to control in a relationship is anger. Couples who are openly enraged with one another may engage in behaviors including shouting, name-calling, constant argumentation, needing to be right all the time, blaming, criticizing, or verbal and physical assault. These behaviors, which are the most overt displays of anger, may be extremely damaging to a relationship and, if they last for a long time, can be challenging to overcome.

- Today, 45-50% of first-time marriages end in divorce. Second and third marriages have a significantly higher rate of divorce.

- Of the 50% of couples who do not divorce, perhaps half are truly happy.

- The major predictor of divorce and marital unhappiness is not disappointment over finances, lack of sexual attraction, or lack of love—it is the way couples manage conflict.

- Verbally and physically abusive couples often inflict long-term pain and suffering on themselves and their children. Verbal or physical violence is part of an estimated one-fourth to one-half of dating relationships.

Less than one in every two marriages today ends in divorce. Although it has decreased slightly over the past five years, the divorce rate is still shockingly high. Only half of the 50% of marriages that do not end in divorce, according to University of Denver psychologist Howard J. Markman, are actually happy. These results imply that American couples lack the abilities necessary to maintain fulfilling marriages.

On a more extreme tangent, around 40-80% of couples who divorce have had one or more incidents of violence or abuse in their relationship. Abusive couples often inflict long-term pain and suffering on themselves and their children. Therefore, out of the subset of unhappy marriages, those couples who are experiencing violence and abuse from one or both partners may need more specific assistance in creating happy, successful marriages than couples who have unhappy marriages but are not violent.

Partner violence has verbal, emotional, financial, and physical forms and couples experiencing issues with violence should seek the guidance of a licensed therapist, psychologist, or counselor.

In spite of the enormous economic and social costs of divorce, there is little long-term research on the causes of marital distress. However, a few studies help us identify some causes.

Markman and Colleagues and John Gottman have separately conducted studies that found that the major predictor of divorce was the way couples handle their disagreements and anger, and the way they communicate and fight about their disappointments. Additionally, John Gottman, a foremost relationship researcher, would add divorce can be predicted from four forms of negative communication found in one or both partners: criticism, defensiveness, stonewalling, and/or contempt. Markman found, and Gottman's research agrees, that couples with the best chance for a successful marriage are those who learn to successfully discuss their problems and when possible, reach solutions.

Unhealthy fighting with one's partner can affect both partners' and their children's mental and physical health. It is important that couples avoid the negative (being defensive, sarcastic, withdrawing) while building positive skills. Long-term studies have found that couples who practice effective communication, anger and conflict management strategies in programs like the Denver-based Prevention and Relationship Enhancement Program see many positive changes. Results include constructive arguing, effective communication, greater relationship satisfaction, fewer sexual problems, fewer instances of physical violence, less dominance, and greater use of problem-solving behaviors.

If learning to manage conflicts is one of the best skills, we can learn to prevent marital distress, divorce, and mental and physical unhealthiness what do we need to know? Please note that when violence and abuse are found in a romantic relationship, that the following skills might not be useful.

CHAPTER 5

MANAGING CONFLICT

There is no one perfect set of rules that is guaranteed to work with every valued relationship. Each couple should use ways that work best to help them talk about problems and try to resolve their issues. Couples can benefit from seeing conflict and frustration as an opportunity for, rather than a failure in, communicating. Try the following skills in your relationship for a month and keep using what works for you.

Skills for Maintaining Positive Communication during Arguments:

1. As a couple, make a commitment to grow both as individuals and as two people in a relationship. Often knowing what one needs to do individually to grow can be difficult and you may want to visit a therapist, counselor, trusted friend, and/or a

spiritual leader to have greater insight into this area.

2. Be aware of your thoughts and emotions throughout all arguments. Realize that you do not need to act in physically or verbally violent ways just because of your feelings and thoughts. Couples have many different arguing styles and the main goal is for both partners to feel safe at all times during the argument and to share their points of view and

emotions with each other to try to reach a solution.

3. Remember, when one partner wins and the other loses in a valued relationship, both lose. The goal of couple's anger and conflict resolution is not to win but to reach a mutually agreeable solution with which you both can live. Competitive couples often like to think of this as letting their relationship win.

4. **Respect** and value yourself and your partner, even when you are angry with her/him. This can be difficult when angry, so when you think a negative thought about your partner, follow it with a positive thought about a skill or characteristic you like about your partner. This will combat the feeling of overall negativity toward your partner so you can maintain respect for each other.

5. During arguments try these skills:

- **Compliment** the positive. "I appreciate your willingness to talk over this issue with me."

- Laugh at yourself. **Humor** can be an effective tension reliever.

- Have a **time-out** rule. If you notice yourself or your partner becoming too angry, then say "I need a time out for 10 minutes. Let's meet in the kitchen after that time." To make an effective time-out, your partner needs to know what is going on (i.e DO NOT just walk away; verbalize the need for a time-out), there needs to be a set time limit on the time out, and each partner needs to know where to meet after the time out to continue the discussion. Taking a time out and never continuing the discussion will make the couple feel as though they never resolve anything. Also, during the time out, each partner needs to do something to cool down and take their mind off the argument – if after the time out period is over and one or both partners are still too upset, then the time out period needs to be extended. NEVER call a time out on your partner, even if they are becoming upset, as this will only serve to increase the negativity in the relationship, simply say "Let's take a time-out."

- Stick to one specific issue at a time. Complaining, griping, or bringing in non-related issues is counterproductive.

  Sometimes partners are trying to communicate their emotions and thoughts when complaining or criticizing – so try focusing on the emotions or thoughts when arguing. For example, if you were to say, "You never pick the children up from their sports activities even though you have tons of time", this is going to come across as a criticism and your partner will just in turn act defensive.

However, if you were to say "I feel hurt and angry that I am the parent who picks up the children from sports activities the majority of the time" then your partner can hear how you feel as she/he is not feeling personally attacked at the same time.

- Share your feelings, thoughts, and needs during the argument. **Use I-statements** rather than you-statements. "I want you to help me set up and follow a monthly budget," rather than, "You always spend money recklessly."

- Ask for and give feedback to see what your partner heard your viewpoint to be and what you heard your partner's viewpoint to be. "It sounds like you're irritated because I bring home my office work. Right?"

- Check out your impressions. "I see a scowl on your face and I sense that you're angry at me. Are you?"

- Respect belt-lines. **Do not hit below the belt** by attacking tender spots and personal vulnerabilities. Avoid statements like, "Gee, for a bald guy, you don't look that old!"

- Ask for what you want—you might just get it! "What I want from you is a commitment to follow a budget for six months."

Also ask your partner, "What do you want from me?"

- Stay in the **here and now**. "What I want from you right now is ___________."

- Talk straight. Say yes when you mean yes and no when you mean no.

- Practice the art of effective **compromise**. Arrive at a solution the two of you can live and experiment with for a month without either of you sabotaging the results.

Anger as An Emotion

At some point or another, everyone has experienced anger. We've all experienced the annoyance and rage that can follow these kinds of events, whether it was because you cut your toe on a table leg, argued with a buddy, or discovered an extra charge on a bill.

When we experience provocation, a danger, a sense of contempt, or just bad luck, anger is typically the emotional reaction. We feel compelled to restrain, resist, or combat the individual or thing that has mistreated or threatened us. The "flight or fight" response causes an increase in our heart rate, blood pressure, and adrenaline levels as an evolutionary byproduct.

Because it gives us a sense of control and authority in a situation where we would otherwise be powerless, this sensation frequently provides consolation or even catharsis. However, this emotion can frequently get out of hand, especially in interpersonal and social relationships, and stop people closest to us from offering support or assistance.

Anger With Your Spouse

This identical pattern of emotional reaction typically characterizes anger directed at or in front of your partner. But in a love relationship, the experience and outcomes of expressing this rage can be very different. Every love relationship will probably at some point or another have disagreements or disputes between the parties, and these arguments frequently result in rage on both sides. Conflicts and disputes, however, can swiftly escalate into heated arguments if one person's emotions is unrestrained or poorly controlled.

A person's constant and unrestrained anger can frequently leave the other person feeling angry, hurt, or overwhelmed. Anger usually breeds more anger. Any kind of connection needs to be able to handle conflicts well, but romantic relationships and good anger management call for it even more.

Managing Anger as a Couple

While anger management is frequently a personal issue, there are times when a group effort is needed to solve the problem. You and your partner can attack the recurrent problem of anger in your relationship as a couple by attending anger management couple's therapy. The approach taken in anger management couples therapy is to view rage as a team dedicated to growing your love and caring for one another through efficient dispute resolution. There are many different methods for managing anger as a couple, including breathing exercises, a self-conscious cognitive approach to what causes the anger, or simply a phrase that makes the angry person more aware of their anger in the moment.

Couples counseling for anger management requires providing them with kind and knowledgeable counselors who will also help you maintain the connection you value.

CHAPTER 6

ANGER MANAGEMENT ADVISE FOR COUPLE

The consequences of your rage depend on how effectively you can control it. Its effects won't be negative if you can control it well. There is a need for good management because rage is going to happen. The following are effective techniques for controlling anger:

1. Avoid The Impulse to Cut Off

Sometimes people who are battling with their significant ones feel the impulse to slam a door and treat them rudely. Going silent will probably make your partner more anxious or angry while temporarily calming you down.

This does not imply that you must sit down and work out a problem right now.

Consider telling your partner that you need some time to collect your thoughts rather than quickly flying out of the driveway or walking away. Tell them that you want to resolve any differences and that you will think about the best period of time to think and then go back to them.

You undoubtedly felt some fear not knowing what would happen if your partner often gives you the silent treatment after you forget an anniversary or skip dinner with their parents. Although you can't force others to talk to you, you can let them know that you're willing to collaborate and share your ideas when they're ready. They're likely to cut off even more if you try to quickly reconcile them under duress or danger.

2. Focus On Managing Yourself

When someone we care about is upset with us, we frequently feel compelled to calm them down as soon as we can. But in the end, we are only responsible for managing our own thoughts, behaviors, and emotions.

People who can maintain their concentration on controlling their own emotions and reactions allow the other person the room to do the same. Being calm is much more effective than trying to calm someone else. Therefore, consider decreasing your own pulse rate and taking a few deep breaths rather than requesting that they calm down.

3. Be Aware of Triangle

It might be cathartic to vent your anger or annoyance with your partner to a friend, your child, or even your therapist. An emotional triangle is created when we turn to a third party to help us cope with our stress related to another. It's very normal to want to vent, and doing so is not improper.

However, there are occasions when this "triangulating" prevents us from resolving the issue in the initial partnership and can make your spouse feel alone or even more defensive. Therefore, the next time you're angry with your spouse and tempted to call, stop and consider whether you're really looking for advice or just someone to agree with you. If the latter, you might want to try calming down first before asking someone else to do it. And while there is nothing wrong with discussing marital difficulty with your therapist, keep in mind that it is not their job to concur with you that your partner is the antagonist of the story; rather, it is their job to be objective and assist you in doing your best thinking.

4. Look Past the Issue

As people, there are some issues that are likely to elicit an irate or fearful response that may result in confrontation. Topics including money, politics, religion, sex, parenting, or family dysfunction are frequently included.

It's simple to believe that having different beliefs will lead to hostility and conflict, however these emotions are more often the result of our childish responses to these issues than of our actual opinions.

Therefore, return your attention to replying as maturely as you can, rather than getting caught up in ending dispute as soon as possible. This does not imply that you must put up with verbal or physical abuse from a spouse or that you must continue to be in a relationship.

Being willing to not let your emotions completely take over shows that you are mature. It resembles asking, "What would my ideal self be doing in this circumstance?" And you probably won't recognize your best self-slamming doors or yelling at the people you care about.

Remember that you are half of the equation if you feel overpowered by the level of fury in your love relationship. Your relationship will be more mature and calmer if you are more composed. Either you or your partner may decide the relationship isn't suited for you after reaching the same level of maturity. In any case, you're making the decision to control your anger. One is more likely to find a spouse who can make the same decision for them if they are capable

of doing so themselves.

CONCLUSION

Anger does not necessarily mean that your relationship will end badly.

We all experience the emotion of anger, which indicates that action needs to be taken. Experiencing anger alerts, you to a problem. The way you handle your rage can contribute significantly to the issue. Anger can make it nearly impossible for some couples to identify the issue and find a solution.

Most of the time, anger is not the issue in relationships. How partners handle their own anger and how effectively they handle that of their spouse becomes troublesome.